Living in
Jamaica

Written and photographed
by Judy Bastyra

SEA-TO-SEA

Mankato Collingwood London

This edition first published in 2007 by
Sea-to-Sea Publications
1980 Lookout Drive
North Mankato
Minnesota 56003

Printed in China

Library of Congress Cataloging-in-Publication Data
Bastyra, Judy.
    Jamaica / by Judy Bastyra.
      p. cm. -- (Living in--)
    Includes index.
    ISBN-13: 978-1-59771-047-3
    1. Jamaica--Juvenile literature. 2. Jamaica--Social life and customs--Juvenile
literature. I. Title. II. Series.

F1868.2.B38 2006
972.92--dc22

2005057111

9 8 7 6 5 4 3 2

Published by arrangement with the Watts Publishing Group Ltd, London
Series editor: Ruth Thomson
Series designer: Edward Kinsey
Consultant: Karen Carpenter, Lecturer in Psychology, University of the
West Indies

Additional photographs: Eye Ubiquitous: cover, 6(c), 19(l), 20(c), 23(l);
James Davis Worldwide: 8(c); Jamaican Information Service: 28(l and r);
Jamaican Tourist Board: 5(br), 9(tl), 13(bl), 14(tl and bl); Cookie
Kinkaid: title page, 8(br), 9(tr); Half Moon Hotel: 4(c); J. Wray and
Nephew 15(tr and br); David Hampton: 3, 10(c), 13(br), 17(tr, bl, br),
21(br), 24(tr,br), 25, 27(br), 28 (tr), 29(tr, br), 30.

The author would like to thank the following people
and organizations for their help with this book:
Mavis Belasse, Bunny, Virginia Burke, Marilyn
Delevante, Carl Dennis, Mike Dennis, Ryan
Douglas, The Excelsior Preprimary and Primary
schools, The Gleaner, Peta-Vonne and Yvonne
Golding, Venise Green, The Jamaican Information
Service in London, The Jamaican Tourist Board,
Junior Lodge, Ele Rickhams, St. Teresa's Prep.
School, Maxine Shroder, Carmen Tipling, Beverley
White, Evan Williams.

Contents

This is Jamaica

Jamaica is an island in the Caribbean Sea, south of Cuba and west of Haiti.

It has numerous mountains, rivers, waterfalls, and beaches, as well as forests and woodlands. Its original name, *Xaymaca*, means "land of wood and water."

△**The Blue Mountains** Coffee is grown on these mountains just north of Kingston.

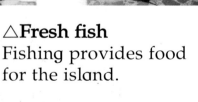

△**Fresh fish** Fishing provides food for the island.

▷**Half Moon Bay** The island's wide, sandy beaches attract more than one million tourists each year.

Fact Box
Capital: Kingston
Population: almost 3 million— a further 2.5 million live overseas
Official Languages: English and Jamaican Creole (Patois)
Main religion: Christianity
Highest mountain: Blue Mountains Peak (7,401 ft/2,256 m)
Longest river: Black River (43 miles/70 km)
Biggest city: Kingston
Currency: Jamaican dollar

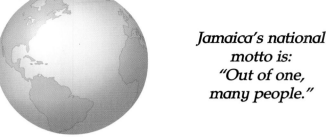

Jamaica's national motto is: "Out of one, many people."

▷**Bamboo Avenue**
Bamboo grows well in Jamaica's tropical climate.

Montego Bay •

• St. Ann's Bay

Dunn's River Falls •

Great River

Blue Lagoon •

BLUE MOUNTAINS

GREAT MORASS

• Mandeville

Black River •

May Pen •

Spanish Town •

▲ Blue Mountains Peak

Kingston •

Caribbean Sea

NORTH AMERICA

Atlantic Ocean

CUBA

HAITI

DOMINICAN REPUBLIC

JAMAICA

Caribbean Sea

Pacific Ocean

SOUTH AMERICA

▷**St. Ann's Bay**
There are sheltered bays and coves all along the north coast. In 1494, the explorer Christopher Columbus landed at this bay, looking for gold.

Kingston–the capital

Kingston, the capital of Jamaica, is a big city that sprawls along the southeast coast. It is bordered on two sides by the Blue Mountains.

The city is home to the government, big businesses, banks, major stores, and theaters. It also has one of the world's largest deep-water harbors.

△**Soldiers**
Soldiers help the police keep the peace in times of emergency.

△**Downtown**
Downtown is the center of Kingston and the old city. Many people work in offices here.

◁**New Kingston**
New Kingston is a business district, with modern high-rise hotels, banks, and office buildings, as well as houses.

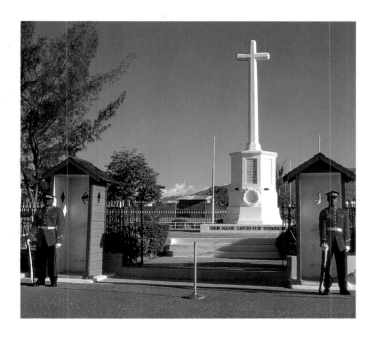

◁Heroes' Park

This memorial honors soldiers who fought alongside the British in the two World Wars (1914-18 and 1939-45).

▷National heroes

Other memorials in the park honor Bustamante, Nanny, Bogle, Sharp, Manley, Garvey, and Gordon—Jamaica's seven national heroes.

Sir Alexander Bustamante, Jamaica's first Prime Minister

◁Devon House

George Stiebel, Jamaica's first black millionaire, built this home in 1740. It is now a museum with stores, an ice-cream parlor, and restaurants in the grounds.

7

Famous sights

The famous sights of Jamaica are both natural and historic. The Spanish came to Jamaica in 1494. The British captured the island in 1655 and brought African slaves to work on their tobacco and sugar plantations. They ruled until independence in 1962.

Several plantation houses are now museums and show how both slaves and plantation managers lived.

△Heritage Park
This life-sized model of an Afro-Jamaican house is made of wattle and daub. It is in the Maima Seville Great House and Heritage Park.

▷Port Royal
This town was the pirate capital of the Caribbean. It was once the richest place in the New World. It was destroyed by an earthquake in 1692.

△Rose Hall
The most famous plantation house in Jamaica has been restored to its original state. A witch is said to haunt it.

◁Blue Lagoon

This very deep lagoon is fed by freshwater springs. It changes color, from deep blue to intense green, all through the day.

▷Dunn's River Falls

This is the largest, most famous of the numerous falls that are found on the island. Many international movies are filmed here.

◁Animal and bird life

About 300 crocodiles live by the mangroves (tropical trees) in the Black River. More than 100 species of birds live in the wetlands of the Great Morass that surround the river.

Living in cities

There are two large cities in Jamaica—Kingston and Montego Bay. One-third of the population lives in Kingston. Montego Bay, a much smaller city, is a tourist resort on the north coast. It has some of the most luxurious hotels and stores on the island. Many Jamaicans find work here in the tourist industry.

Jamaican stamps

◁△**The post office**
There are very few mailboxes, so people send letters from the post office. They can pick up mail here as well, from their own, individual mailbox.

◁**Tivoli Gardens**
This area of housing is one of the most dangerous places in Kingston. There are often fights here between local gangs.

▽**Water hydrants**
Water hydrants are a common sight all over Kingston. The fire department uses them in emergencies.

▽Office work

The head offices of major industries, such as banks, insurance, distilleries, mining, and cement and flour mills are found in Kingston.

Working in the city

Country people are increasingly moving to the cities to find work. Young people come to learn a trade, or to work in offices, hotels, and hospitals.

△Street selling

In many areas of town, street traders sell food they have bought from farmers.

▷Pan chicken

Cooked chicken is sold by the roadside. It is grilled over charcoal in converted oil drums.

Living in the country

Jamaicans call anywhere outside the cities "country." Some villages are tiny and remote. Others, on main roads, have a church, a general store, and a bar. When Jamaicans return to the island after many years working abroad, they usually build their new homes in the countryside.

△Squatting
People often live in houses on abandoned land that doesn't belong to them. This is called "squatting on captured land."

▷Village houses
In the country, there is space for people to add on new rooms to their houses, as their family grows in size.

△Chattel house
Village houses are often made of wood. The overhanging verandah gives shade from the sweltering sun.

▷Clothes washing

Not all country people have running water. They wash their clothes in a nearby stream or river.

▽The market

Once a week, country people go to their nearest market to buy food, clothes, and household goods.

"Picka-peppa" sauce

Honey

Hot pepper sauce

Tinned ackee (tropical fruit)

Tropical fruit sticks

Cookies

Guava jelly

△A village store

Village stores sell lots of different items, such as canned and packaged foods, as well as kerosine and matches.

Working in the country

In the country, people raise sheep, cows, and goats or grow crops, such as bananas, sugarcane, coffee, and vegetables. Some people mine bauxite, used to make aluminum, or work in food or drink factories. Hotels, restaurants, and tourist attractions on the coast employ a great many people, too.

△Vegetable farming

Vegetables are grown to sell locally. Some restaurants and hotels pay farmers to grow certain vegetables, such as bell peppers and zucchini.

▷Goat rearing

Farmers raise goats for their meat. Curry goat and *mannish water* (goat broth) are both very popular dishes.

◁Bananas

Bananas are grown as a cash crop. They are picked before they are fully ripe. They turn yellow as they ripen, on their way to other countries.

▽Village crafts

Some villages earn a living though crafts. This village makes handmade brooms with palm leaves and wood from local trees.

Country industries

Food and drink processing factories are mainly in the country, near where the crops are produced. These provide jobs for local people.

△Sugarcane

Sugarcane is an important crop. The cane is pressed to extract its juice. This is fermented and made into rum or vodka.

▷Rum barrels

Rum is put into barrels and left for several years to age, before it is bottled. Rum is an important Jamaican export.

Shopping

Every city and town has a market, which takes place daily or weekly. Many places also have a supermarket. In the cities, there are indoor shopping malls and plazas, where a number of small stores are grouped around a parking lot. In tourist areas, there are fashionable boutiques selling clothes and souvenirs.

△**Coconut water**
Roadside coconut sellers cut off the top of green coconuts, so people can drink the water inside.

▷**Fresh peas**
This farmer has brought his gungo peas to sell on the street. Behind him, another street seller (*higgler*) has laid out clothes to sell.

▽**Hubcaps**
Jamaicans like making their cars look stylish. Hubcaps are often sold in the open air, like this.

△**Pots and pans**
These traditional, heavy "Dutchy" cooking pots are made in Jamaica.

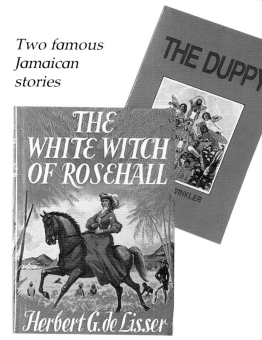

Two famous Jamaican stories

△**A furniture store**
Courts is the largest furniture store in Jamaica. It has branches all over the island. It also helps to raise money for schools.

△**A bookshop**
Bookshops import books from North America and Britain, as well as selling books published in Jamaica.

▽**Fabric**
Many people in Jamaica make their own clothes. They buy material and thread at fabric shops.

△**Jamaican money**
Jamaica's currency is dollars and cents.

On the move

Not everywhere on the island can be reached by car. It can take many hours to drive from one place to another, because most roads are so twisty.

Jamaicans drive on the left. They have a saying to remind visitors, "Keep left and you'll always be right."

△Motorbikes
Motorbikes are a popular form of transportation. People often give others a ride.

▷Country roads
There are more than 9,320 miles (15,000 km) of roads, but only 25% of them are paved. Many have potholes after heavy rains.

▷New roads
New roads have helped ease the traffic jams to and from the capital.

◁**Bus transportation**
Every town has a bus waiting area, usually near the main market or shopping center.

▽**Cars**
Many people own cars. They buy inexpensive, used cars from abroad.

Buses and railroads

A bus network links virtually every village in the country. Air-conditioned express buses carry office workers to and from Kingston. Slower, but less expensive, buses stop more frequently.

Jamaica used to have a passenger railroad, but trains are now used only to transport bauxite to the port.

Religion

Religion plays an important role in the Jamaican way of life. Most Jamaicans are Christian. Each weekend, families go to church together to pray and meet their friends from the same parish. There are many different kinds of church in each parish, such as Baptist, Methodist, and Seventh-Day Adventist.

△**Going to church**
People dress in their best clothes to go to church.

△**Saying grace**
Families often say grace at mealtimes, thanking God for providing their food.

◁**Church services**
Singing is an important part of church services. Many churches have choirs. In this service someone is being baptized.

△Seventh-Day Adventists

These Christians believe in a very simple life, good food, and regular exercise. Their holy day lasts from sundown on Friday until sundown on Saturday.

◁▽Rasta hats

Rastafarians twist their hair into long lengths called dreadlocks as a symbol of their beliefs. A rasta hat is larger than usual, in order to cover the dreadlocks.

△▷Rastafarians

Rastafarians believe that the late emperor of Ethiopia, Haile Selassie, is their living God.

The teachings of Haile Selassie

A Rasta hat (a tam)

A CD by Bob Marley, the Reggae singer, Jamaica's most famous Rastafarian

21

Family life

In Jamaica, everyone related to you is considered part of your close family. Although some fathers and mothers do not live together, everyone in the family helps bring up the children. Sometimes, when their parents go abroad to work, children are looked after by grandmothers and aunties.

△**Children**
Children are considered a great blessing. The more children you have, the more blessed you are.

◁**Extended families**
Some families include three generations living together.

◁Rastafarians

Rastafarian women are expected to be modest and humble.

▷Close families

Many families live near their relatives. Cousins often play together.

Working mothers

Many women go out to work as well as bringing up their family. Those who can afford it employ helpers to run their homes and look after the children until they come home from work.

◁Fathers

Fathers play an active role in their children's lives. Fathers not married to their children's mothers are known as "baby fathers."

23

Time to eat

No one in Jamaica need ever go hungry. Plenty of fruit and vegetables grow in the fertile island soil. There is always a good supply of fish, chicken, and pork. Most Jamaicans eat three hearty meals a day and one of them always includes rice.

They also drink a great many fresh fruit juices and nourishing food supplements.

Bammies

△**A fish dish**
Fried fish with hot peppers, onion rings, and cassava bread (*bammy*) is sold by roadsides near the sea.

◁▽**Patties**
Patties are the national snack. These crescent-shaped pies are filled with ground beef, chicken, or shrimp.

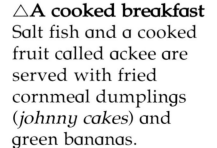

△**A cooked breakfast**
Salt fish and a cooked fruit called ackee are served with fried cornmeal dumplings (*johnny cakes*) and green bananas.

Juici Patties
...and so much more

A patty

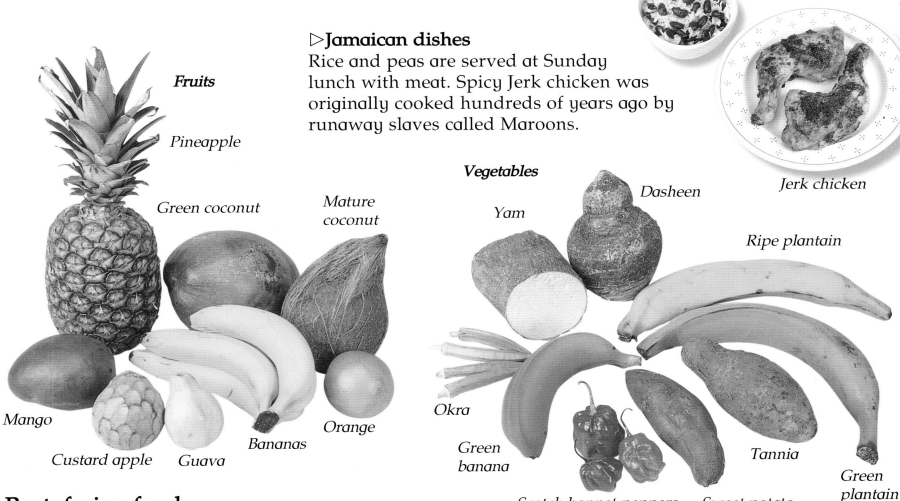

Rice and peas

▷Jamaican dishes

Rice and peas are served at Sunday lunch with meat. Spicy Jerk chicken was originally cooked hundreds of years ago by runaway slaves called Maroons.

Jerk chicken

Fruits

Pineapple

Green coconut

Mature coconut

Mango

Custard apple   *Guava*

Bananas

Orange

Vegetables

Yam

Dasheen

Ripe plantain

Okra

Green banana

Scotch bonnet peppers

Sweet potato

Tannia

Green plantain

Rastafarian food

The Rastafarians have their own style of cooking, called Ital. They are vegetarian and do not use many seasonings or salt. They believe in eating fresh, pure food.

◁Bun and cheese

A common Jamaican snack is a sandwich made of a spiced bun and processed cheese.

School time

Jamaicans value education highly. Children have to go to school up to the age of 15. Some Jamaican families who live abroad have begun sending their children back to the island to be educated. They feel that schooling in Jamaica is better than elsewhere.

△Walk to school
Most children who live in the country walk to school. The older children walk with their younger sisters or brothers.

△School hours
School starts at 8 a.m. and finishes at 1.30 p.m. At about 10 a.m., children wash their hands outside before their midmorning snack.

◁The school
The classrooms at this school are built around a shady courtyard.

◁**School uniform**
Every school has
a school uniform.
Children wear a
separate uniform
for sports.

▷**Classroom**
There are between 20
and 30 children to a
class. Both a teacher
and a student teacher
teach many of the
lessons.

Further education

Many pupils go onto
further education after
secondary school, because
this will help them get a
better job. They may go
to a technical college, a
teacher's training college,
or to one of the
universities in Kingston.

△**Religious education**
Children are taught how
to behave. Sometimes
bible stories are used.

△**Reading books**
English books include
many poems and
stories written about
Jamaica.

Having fun

Jamaicans spend their leisure time on the beach, playing, watching sports, watching TV, going to the movies, and listening to music.

No party is complete without dancing to the sound of Reggae music, which started in Jamaica.

▷**The lottery**
The lottery is so popular that it is drawn twice a week.

▽**Dance**
Jamaicans are very proud of their dance and music traditions.

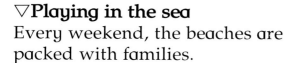

▽**Playing in the sea**
Every weekend, the beaches are packed with families.

◁Cricket

Many boys want to become cricketers. If they cannot afford the real equipment, they make their own bat and use a small coconut as a cricket ball.

△The Reggae Boyz

Jamaicans are enthusiastic supporters of their national soccer team, the Reggae Boyz.

◁Soccer

Playing soccer is a favorite pastime for young Jamaican boys.

△*The Children's Own*

This children's newspaper, written partly by children, is sent to schools throughout Jamaica.

29

Going further

Bob Marley

Bob Marley is Jamaica's most famous musician. There is a museum about him in Kingston. He died some years ago, but his music is still very popular.

Either listen to his music or read his lyrics and then design a Bob Marley CD cover. You can find out more about him at www.bobmarley.com.

Colorful birds

Because it is an island, Jamaica has many bird species not found anywhere else in the world. Choose a bird from www.babybirdcalendar.com/jamaica.html and write a report about it. Describe what it looks like, its feeding and nesting habits, and its habitat.

Treasure hunt

The fierce pirate, Captain Henry Morgan, buried some of his treasure in Jamaica.

Draw a map of Jamaica and mark the place where you think his treasure might be.

Websites

www.jamaicans.com/childsguide/index.shtml

www.yahooligans.yahoo.com/around_the_world (type Jamaica into the box and click on "search")

Glossary

Aluminum A light silvery metal, often used to make tinfoil or drinks cans.

Cash crop A crop that is grown for sale and not as food for a farmer.

Currency The money used by a country.

Distillery A place where alcohol is made.

Dreadlocks A hairstyle worn by Rastafarians, where long hair is twisted into tight braids.

Fermented Turned into alcohol.

Kerosine A paraffin oil used for heating and lamps.

Lagoon An area of sheltered coastal water separated from the sea by a sandbank or a coral reef.

New World The continents of North and South America and the islands around them, including those in the Caribbean. When Europeans first came to these places, it was like finding a new world.

Parish A Jamaican term for one of the 12 subdivisions of the country's three counties, which are Cornwall, Middlesex, and Surrey.

Patois (Patwa) One of Jamaica's two languages, also known as Jamaican Creole. It is a mixture of Spanish, English, and African languages.

Plantation Land planted with a single crop, such as coffee, sugarcane, or bananas.

Population The total number of people living in a place.

Reggae music Popular music of the West Indies.

Slave A person who is legally owned by another.

Tropical Of the Tropics, the hot and often wet regions either side of the Equator, the imaginary line that runs around the Earth at its middle.

Wattle and daub A woven network of twigs covered with mud or clay, used for building.

Wetlands Swamps and other damp areas of land.

Index